THE
CHRISTIAN
COUNSELOR'S

THE CHRISTIAN COUNSELOR'S

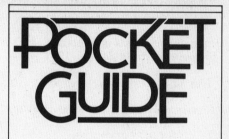

POCKET GUIDE

Selwyn Hughes

BETHANY HOUSE PUBLISHERS
MINNEAPOLIS, MINNESOTA 55438
A Division of Bethany Fellowship, Inc.

The Christian Counselor's Pocket Guide
Copyright © 1980, 1985
Selwyn Hughes

Originally published in England by
Crusade for World Revival, 1977

This edition expanded, revised

Library of Congress Catalog Card Number 80–65443

ISBN 0–87123–844–6

Published by Bethany House Publishers
A Ministry of Bethany Fellowship International
11400 Hampshire Avenue South
Minneapolis, Minnesota 55438
www.bethanyhouse.com

Printed in the United States of America by
Bethany Press International
Minneapolis, Minnesota 55438

About the Author

Selwyn Hughes is the founder/director of Crusade for World Revival. He has been a minister for over 25 years, and has given a great deal of time to the area of personal counseling. He is currently involved in the training of Christian counselors in Britain.

● Be sure to use the abilities God has given you. Keep a close watch on all you do and think. Stay true to what is right and God will bless you and use you to help others.

—1 Timothy 4:14–16
The Living Bible

A Counselor?
. . . Who? . . . Me?

HELPING people with their problems is not just the task of professional counselors—it is the commission of every Christian also. Whether we realize it or not, almost all of us are involved in counseling situations every day of our lives. A friend has a problem in his marriage; a neighbor has lost a loved one; a relative has discovered that she has cancer; a son or daughter has to be talked to about their unacceptable behavior—all these are counseling situations demanding insight, sympathy and personal concern.

One does not need to be a professional counselor, or to have received specialized training, in order to help people with their problems. It is true, of course, that some people are supernaturally gifted by God for this purpose, as explained in Romans 12:6–8: "Through the grace of God we have different gifts . . . and if our gift be the stimulating of the faith of others, let us set ourselves to it" (Phillips). This gift of "stimulating the faith of others" is the God-given ability to help uncover and resolve the deep problems which hinder Christians in their spiritual growth and progress toward spiritual maturity. You might now be saying, "Well, I'm not conscious of having a special gift in counseling so that lets me out." It doesn't! Even though you may not have a particular spiritual gift for dealing with in-depth problems, every Christian is commanded by God to have a practical and sacrificial concern for others. James tells us, "Now what use is it, my brothers, for a man to say he 'has faith' if his actions do not correspond with it?" (James 2:14, Phillips). A similar thought is expressed in Philippians 2:4: "Don't just think about your own affairs, but be interested in others, too, and in what they are doing" (TLB). In 1 Thessalonians 5:11 we are told to "encourage each other to build each other up" (TLB), and in Galatians 6:2 we are commanded to "share each other's troubles and problems, and so obey the Lord's command" (TLB).

The New Testament encourages every Christian to assume the responsibility for one another's spiritual development, and to help toward that end, this booklet has been compiled. Recent studies have shown that Christian laymen and nonprofessional counselors are sometimes more effective in helping people with their problems than those with long years of specialized training. A survey conducted by Robert Karkhuff on the results of a research into comparisons between professional and lay counselors indicated that the counselees of lay counselors improved as well as (and in some cases better than) the counselees of the professionals. This conclusion does not invalidate the need for specialized training in counseling, but it does show that those who are untrained and have a genuine desire to help others can bring about great changes in the lives of those with whom they counsel.

O. H. Mowrer, one time president of the American Psychological Association, in his book *The Crisis in Psychiatry and Religion*, has openly challenged the view that only professionally trained counselors should handle in-depth problems. He claims that Christian laymen can bring a healing spiritual dimension into the lives of those who are seriously troubled and disturbed that no secular counselor or therapist could match.

The question is often asked, "How does Christian counseling differ from secular counseling?" In two ways: (1) Christian counseling is largely *directive*, as opposed to the nondirective approach of secular counselors, and (2) it makes great use of the Bible. Much of modern-day counseling is nondirective in that it encourages the counselee to look within himself for the solutions to his problem. Christian counseling seeks to bring the principles of God's Word, the Bible, to bear upon human problems, and there are times in the counseling process when the best thing one can do for the counselee is to read him what God says about the matter in the Scriptures. Christian counseling is therefore *telling people, with deep compassion and genuine love, what God requires of them.*

We are told in 2 Timothy 3:16 that the breath of God has gone into the compilation of the Bible and it is, therefore, a *God-breathed book.* "All scripture is given by inspiration [or the breath] of God, and is profitable for doctrine, for reproof, for correction, for instruction in righteousness." We see also that the breath of God has gone into the creation of man, "And the Lord God breathed into his nostrils the breath of life: and man became a living soul" (Gen. 2:7). The same breath that went into the making of man has gone into the making of the Bible, for it was God's intention that the Scriptures should become the reference book for man's continued spiritual and psychological development on this earth. Along with the product (man) God has provided a *Manufacturer's Handbook* (the Bible) which contains all the principles necessary to a happy and successful life in this world and the world to come.

Caution

Finally, a word of caution. One of the most important aspects of counseling, whether it is dealing with in-depth problems or simply sharing spiritual advice, is to know when to refer. This is a matter that cannot be too strongly emphasized. You should always be ready to refer the person you are counseling to someone more experienced than yourself whenever you feel that the problem is outside the limits of your own insight or experience. Watch out for the following signs which tell you to consider introducing the person you are counseling to a minister, or an appropriate professional person:

- when a person has severe depression, or remains suicidal even after your best efforts to help.
- when you lack the physical or spiritual stamina to deal with the problem.
- when the person arouses strong feelings of dislike in you.
- when the person requires medical attention.

- when the person has serious financial difficulties.

The person will not feel rejected when referred to someone else if you preface your remarks with the statement, "I want to help you, but your problem is beyond the limits of my ability and experience. Therefore I would like to introduce you to someone whose experience is greater than mine in this matter and who will, I feel sure, be able to help you much better than I."

May God bless you as you give yourself to the task of bringing about a spiritual change in the lives of those to whom God leads you to counsel.

THE winning of a soul to Jesus Christ is the greatest joy known to man. Unfortunately, comparatively few Christians are equipped to deal with earnest inquirers, and fewer still are able to answer the honest doubts of a seeking soul.

The following section deals with twelve questions often asked by the unconverted, and contains also some helpful suggestions and scripture references to use when dealing with these problems.

These suggestions are not given in order that you might demonstrate to the unconverted your intellectual or spiritual superiority. No one is won into the Kingdom of God by being beaten in an argument. Be loving, persuasive, and share the truth with a genuine concern for the other person's spiritual well-being.

"If anybody asks why you believe as you do, be ready to tell him, and do it in a gentle and respectful way" (1 Pet. 3:15, TLB).

Difficulties of the unconverted

● Bible References

"Though your sins be as scarlet. . . ."
(ISA. 1:18)

"The Son of man is come to seek and to save. . . ."
(LUKE 19:10)

"I am not come to call the righteous, but sinners. . . ."
(MATT. 9:13)

"Christ Jesus came into the world to save sinners; of whom I am chief."
(1 TIM. 1:15)

"For whosoever shall call upon the name of the Lord shall be saved."
(ROM. 10:13)

"Whosoever believeth in him shall receive remission of sins."
(ACTS 10:43)

"Behold the Lamb of God, which taketh away the sin of the world."
(JOHN 1:29)

I am too great a sinner

When helping anyone who has made a statement like this, never give the impression that
his sins are *not* great. Sin is an offense against
God and should never be minimized. Say something like this: "There can be no doubt that our
holy God looks upon sin as repulsive, but He
loves each one of us with an unconditional love.
Therefore, He devised a way by which *every* sin
can be forgiven." Open your Bible to Isaiah 53:6
and invite the person you are dealing with to
read the verse out loud. Then ask the question:
"What does this verse say God has done with
sin?" The answer is quite plain—He has laid it
upon Christ. If the person is slow in seeing this
truth or hesitant to respond, use the following
illustration. "Let this Bible represent your sin,
my left hand represent you, and my right hand
represent Christ." Place your Bible on your left
hand and ask the person: "Where is your sin
now?" Encourage him to answer: "On me." Then
place the Bible on your right hand (the hand
which represents Christ) and ask: "Where is
your sin now?" The answer, of course, is: "The
sin is on Christ." Next, point the person to scriptures on the opposite page which show that
Christ has paid the penalty for *every* human sin.
John 1:29 and Acts 10:43 are particularly helpful here. Another helpful insight is to show the
person that although he thinks himself to be a
great sinner, he cannot claim to be the *greatest*
sinner. Paul claimed that in 1 Timothy 1:15. If
the *greatest* sinner has been saved, then salvation is possible to every other human being.

● Bible References

"Seek ye first the kingdom of God."

(MATT. 6:33)

"Behold, now is the accepted time; behold, now is the day of salvation."

(2 COR. 6:2)

"But God said unto him, Thou fool, this night shall thy soul be required of thee."

(LUKE 12:20)

"Walk while ye have the light, lest darkness come upon you."

(JOHN 12:35)

"Whereas you know not what shall be on the morrow."

(JAMES 4:13)

"Strive to enter in at the strait gate: for many, I say unto you, will seek to enter in, and shall not be able."

(LUKE 13:24)

I'll decide sometime

A good verse to use with someone in this position is Isaiah 55:6. Invite the person to read the verse aloud and then pose the question: "*When* should we seek the Lord?" When he answers: "While he may be found," ask *when* that is. The person will usually be perplexed at this point; use the moment to show that no one has a guarantee on tomorrow. Death, natural disasters and accidents all make life uncertain. Ask him: "Can you be sure of finding Christ tomorrow if you do not seek Him today?" Another useful verse when a person procrastinates is Proverbs 29:1. Once again, get the person to read the verse aloud. Ask the question: "What becomes of the one who 'being often reproved hardeneth his neck'?" When the answer is given: "He shall suddenly be destroyed," bear down on this point. Encourage the person not to take risks with the important issue of eternal salvation. Dr. Chalmers, a famous evangelist, used to use the following method when dealing with procrastinators. He would say: "Are you willing to wait a year with no opportunity under any circumstances, no matter what comes up, to accept Christ?" When the person answered: "No, I might die within a year," Dr. Chalmers would then say: "Well, would you be willing to wait a month?" Next he would bring it down to a week, and then a day, saying, "Would you like God to leave you alone for a day with no opportunity, under any circumstances, of accepting Christ?" Dr. Chalmers won many people to Christ following this method. So can you.

● Bible References

"Who are kept by the power of God through faith unto salvation. . . ."

(1 PET. 1:5)

"Now unto him that is able to keep you from falling. . . ."

(JUDE 24)

"Christ liveth in me."

(GAL. 2:20)

"He is able to keep."

(2 TIM. 1:12)

"My sheep . . . follow me . . . and I give unto them eternal life."

(JOHN 10:27, 28)

"God is able to make him stand."

(ROM. 14:4)

"But the Lord is faithful, who shall stablish you."
(2 THESS. 3:3)

I could never keep it up

Point out to the person who presents this problem that no one can live a truly Christian life in his own strength. Trying to live a good life without God is rebellion against Him. Christ has to live His life in us and through us or else we have no life at all. Take a pencil in your right hand and place it vertically on your left palm. Take your hand away. The pencil will, of course, fall over. Do this several times and then press home the point that only Christ is able to uphold us and "keep [us] from falling" (Jude 24). Explain that when a person becomes a Christian, he receives from Christ a special supply of God's power which enables him to live in the strength of Christ himself. Go on to say that the Christian religion is the only religion in the world whose founder came back from the dead to live His life in the personalities of His followers. John 10:28, 29 shows beautifully that the safety of the person who accepts Christ does not depend on that person's ability to hang on, but upon the keeping power of the Father and the Son. Second Timothy 1:12 also shows that it is Christ's business and not ours to keep that which is entrusted to Him and that He is well able to do it. First Corinthians 10:13 is extremely helpful for a person who is afraid that some strong temptation will overcome him and he will fall. Emphasize to the person that the Christian life does not rest in his ability, but in his response to Christ's ability.

● Bible References

"There is none righteous, no, not one."
(ROM. 3:10)

"All we like sheep have gone astray."
(ISA. 53:6)

"For as many as are of the works of the law are under the curse."
(GAL. 3:10)

"But as many as received him to them gave he power to become the sons of God."
(JOHN 1:12)

"If thou shalt confess with thy mouth the Lord Jesus, and shalt believe in thine heart that God hath raised him from the dead, thou shalt be saved."
(ROM. 10:9)

"Except ye be converted, and become as little children, ye shall not enter into the kingdom of heaven."
(MATT. 18:3)

I've always believed in Jesus

This is regarded as the most common objection and difficulty among people who have not experienced a genuine conversion. A person who makes this statement is entertaining a false hope if he merely believes in Jesus as a historical figure. Take the person through the basic steps of salvation and show him that in order to be saved and have a guaranteed place in heaven, one must have a *personal* encounter with Jesus Christ. This means knowing *Him* as distinct from knowing *about* Him. Explain these simple steps: (1) Ever since Adam and Eve's original transgression in the Garden of Eden, every man and woman born into this world has sinned (Isa. 53:6; Rom. 3:23). (2) Since God cannot allow sin in heaven, He provided a way whereby sin could be forgiven, through the death of His own Son on the cross (Rom. 5:6, 8). (3) It is not enough that Christ has died; to experience forgiveness one must appropriate the benefits of His death by personally repenting of sin and receiving Christ into one's life as Lord and Savior (Rom. 10:9; Acts 3:19). You will need to make clear to this person the difference between head belief and heart belief. For example, a person may believe a plane is safe but still be unwilling to travel on it. His belief is merely in his head. Similarly, no one can truly experience Christ's provision of salvation until he is willing to commit himself to it fully and completely.

4

● Bible References

"The Lord is . . . not willing that any should perish."

(2 PET. 3:9)

"And ye will not come to me, that ye might have life."

(JOHN 5:40)

"As I live, saith the Lord God, I have no pleasure in the death of the wicked."

(EZEK. 33:11)

"He that believeth not the Son shall not see life."
(JOHN 3:36)

"Except ye repent, ye shall all likewise perish."
(LUKE 13:3)

"If ye believe not that I am he, ye shall die in your sins."

(JOHN 8:24)

God is too good to damn anyone

This person needs to be shown that the same Bible which tells of God's goodness also points out another ingredient in His character—justice. As a just God, He has to punish sin. He must protect His kingdom of goodness. The scriptures opposite show that it is not so much God who damns men and women as their damning themselves by rejecting God's offer of mercy and forgiveness as expressed through the cross. God's goodness is seen in the way He provides us with salvation from the consequences of our sin—which is hell. Read Romans 2:4, 5 to the person and say something like this: "Now you can see from what God says here that the purpose of His goodness is to lead you to repentance, not to encourage you to sin." John 8:21, 24 and John 3:16 show clearly that however much God loves us, He will most certainly reject those who reject His Son. You can also say, "You see, God is not willing that anyone should perish, and He offers the gift of eternal life to you, but there is one difficulty in the way. Would you like to know what it is?" When the person replies, refer him to John 5:40 to see what the difficulty is. The passage reads, "Ye will not come to me that ye might have life." You can conclude by saying lovingly and compassionately: "In Christ, God offers you forgiveness for your sin and the gift of eternal life. If you won't accept it, then God has no other alternative but to allow you to perish."

● Bible References

"Thou art inexcusable . . . whosoever thou art that judgest."

(ROM. 2:1)

"First cast out the beam out of thine own eye."
(MATT. 7:1–5)

"Thus saith the Lord, What iniquity have your fathers found in me?"

(JER. 2:5)

"If ye forgive not men their trespasses, neither will your Father forgive your trespasses."
(MATT. 6:15)

"Forgiving one another, even as God for Christ's sake hath forgiven you."

(EPH. 4:32)

"Peter . . . said, Lord, how oft shall my brother sin against me, and I forgive him? till seven times? Jesus saith unto him . . . until seventy times seven."

(MATT. 18:21–22)

There are too many hypocrites

This argument is usually advanced by those who have been mistreated in some way by a professing Christian. Encourage the person to talk about this; ventilating the problem will make it easier for him to receive what you have to say. Using Romans 14:4 and 12, show him that he is solely responsible for his own relationship with God, and what others do bears little relation to the issue. Turn the person's attention from how others have treated him to how God has treated him. Jeremiah 2:5, Isaiah 53:5 and Romans 5:6–8 are useful for this purpose. Ask the person: "If a Christian has treated you badly, is this any excuse for you to reject a heavenly Father who has treated you with such tenderness and concern?" Confronting a man using this excuse, an evangelist opened his Bible and read Jeremiah 2:5: "Thus saith the Lord, What iniquity have your fathers found in me, that they are gone far from me, and have walked after vanity, and are become vain?" He then said: "Did you find any iniquity in God? Has not God treated you well?" The man admitted that the Almighty had not treated him badly and responded to the evangelist's invitation to receive Christ. Point out also that it is only when we are prepared to forgive others who have hurt us that we can fully experience God's forgiveness. Matthew 18:23–25, Ephesians 4:30–32 and Matthew 6:14–15 can be used effectively when attempting to do this.

6

● Bible References

"For God took the sinless Christ and poured into him our sins. Then, in exchange, he poured God's goodness into us."

(2 COR. 5:21, TLB)

"Repent ye . . . for the kingdom of heaven is at hand."

(MATT. 3:2)

"God . . . commandeth all men everywhere to repent."

(ACTS 17:30)

"And that every tongue should confess that Jesus Christ is Lord."

(PHIL. 2:11)

"The goodness of God leadeth thee to repentance."

(ROM. 2:4)

I tried before but failed

When a person makes this statement, he has probably not experienced a true conversion. A true conversion takes place when a person *repents* of *sin*. If a counselor lacks a clear concept of sin and repentance, any attempt to help a person will prove unproductive. The Bible defines sin as a wrong deed and something deeper. It is allowing life to revolve around ourselves instead of God. Sin rules by keeping self instead of God in the center of our lives. And what is repentance? Repentance is more than being sorry for our wrongdoing. A person can be sorry about his sins and think he has repented, but this is regret, not repentance. Repentance is recognizing that inside us there is a basic self-centeredness that wants its own way. We must firmly remove this self-centeredness by allowing Jesus Christ to come into the spirit, the center of our being, as Savior and Lord. People who invite Christ into a marginal part of their lives and never give Him the center cannot experience a true conversion because the self still rules at the center. Ask the person: "When you invited Christ into your life, did you surrender your self-centeredness and allow Christ to be your Lord?" Sin is really saying to God: "I want to run my life on my own terms." Repentance is saying to God, "Lord, you take over and run my life the way you want it run." Ponder these insights until they are clear to you. Without them you will not be able to help a person experience genuine conversion.

● Bible References

"In thy presence is fulness of joy."

(PS. 16:11)

"He that spared not his own Son . . . how shall he not . . . freely give us all things?"

(ROM. 8:32)

"What shall it profit a man, if he shall gain the whole world, and lose his own soul?"

(MARK 8:36)

"I count all things but loss for the excellency of . . . Christ."

(PHIL. 3:8)

"No good thing will he withhold from them that walk uprightly."

(PS. 84:11)

"The thief cometh not, but for to steal, and to kill, and to destroy: I am come that they might have life, and that they might have it more abundantly."

(JOHN 10:10)

I have too much to give up

Read Mark 8:34–38 with a person who has this problem. Point out that in the matter of one's eternal destiny, it is better by far to give up everything one possesses than to lose one's soul. At the heart of this problem lies a wrong concept of God. The person sees God as someone who wants to take rather than to give. It is part of your counseling to change the person's perspective by focusing on those scriptures that show God to be the generous and magnanimous Giver. Refer the person to Philippians 3:7, 8, which shows that whatever a person gives up for Christ is nothing compared to what he receives from Him. Psalm 84:11 and Romans 8:32 show that God will never ask anyone to give up anything that is helpful to his life, only what is harmful. A young woman once used this argument to an experienced evangelist: "I have too much to give up." He replied, "Do you believe that God loves you?" "Yes," she said, "I believe that." "How much do you think He loves you?" She pondered the question for a little while and said: "He gave His Son to die for me on the cross." "Now," asked the evangelist, "do you really think that if God loved you enough to give His only Son to die for you, He will ask you to give up anything that is good?" The girl saw the point and surrendered her life to Christ that very moment. He asks us to give up only that which, in the long run, would harm us.

● Bible References

"Man shall not live by bread alone, but by every word that proceedeth out of the mouth of God."

(MATT. 4:4)

"For the word of God is quick, and powerful, and sharper than any twoedged sword."

(HEB. 4:12)

"If any of you really determines to do God's will, then you will certainly know whether my teaching is from God."

(JOHN 7:17, TLB)

"But the natural mind receiveth not the things of the Spirit of God . . . because they are spiritually discerned."

(1 COR. 2:14)

"The secret of the Lord is with them that fear him."

(PS. 25:14)

"All scripture is given by inspiration of God."

(2 TIM. 3:16)

I don't believe the Bible

Those who use this argument think that having dismissed the Bible, they can frustrate any attempt on your part to win them to Christ. One approach you can use is to suggest to the person that he would hardly dismiss the world's most important piece of literature without knowing something of its main theme and message. Ask him to summarize its main theme for you. Most people will say "The Golden Rule" or "The Ten Commandments." You can then point out gently and tactfully that the main theme of the Bible is to show us *how we can have eternal life*. Say something like this: "Let me share with you, if I may, what the Bible's main message is." Then proceed to outline the way of salvation. Use Bible passages freely as there is tremendous power in speaking the Word of God to the unconverted. Romans 3:3, 4 is extremely useful to show that questioning a fact does not alter a fact. Second John 10 is a powerful verse to show that a person who does not believe or live by the teachings of Christ is lost. Remember, however, when using texts which are strongly confrontative, do not use them as battering rams to break open a person's heart. Your purpose should not be to win an argument but to win a soul. The text referred to (2 John 10) has been greatly used by the Holy Spirit to convince skeptics of the reliability and authority of God's Word. Present it gently, lovingly and compassionately. It is an awesome responsibility to tell someone he is lost. There should be tears in your voice, if not in your eyes.

9

● Bible References

"He that believeth not the Son . . . the wrath of God abideth on him."

(JOHN 3:36)

"For the wages of sin is death, but the gift of God is eternal life."

(ROM. 6:23)

"Whosoever committeth sin is the servant of sin."

(JOHN 8:34)

"If ye believe not that I am he, ye shall die in your sins."

(JOHN 8:24)

"And whosoever was not found written in the book of life was cast into the lake of fire."

(REV. 20:15)

"And this is the condemnation, that light is come into the world, and men loved darkness rather than light."

(JOHN 3:19)

"He, that being often reproved hardeneth his neck, shall suddenly be destroyed, and that without remedy."

(PROV. 29:1)

I'm not interested in anything religious

Many people reject the concepts of God, Christ, heaven, hell, etc., because accepting them would produce disturbing feelings in their hearts. Instead of facing these feelings, many people reject the thought of anything religious. God has built into every man and woman a conscience, a sensitivity to the laws of God (John 1:9). You can activate the conscience by well-aimed questions. You can ask: *"Do you know that you have committed the greatest sin a person can commit?"* When the person asks you to explain, read Matthew 22:37, 38 and ask him if he has kept the first and greatest commandment. When he says no, point out that to violate the *greatest* commandment is to commit the greatest sin. This question ought *not* to be asked with arrogance or in a jocular manner. Be serious as you present it, asking God to help you break through the person's apparent indifference. Oftentimes, you will meet with someone who is not willing to sit and let you deal with him in the way described above. In that case, the only thing you can do is ask God's guidance in giving the person a short, powerful, pointed verse of scripture. Many evangelists can testify that texts such as Hebrews 10:31 or Romans 6:23, given as a passing shot, have been used by the Holy Spirit to bring a person to Christ. Do not fire these verses as bullets from your spiritual gun; share them wisely, lovingly and compassionately.

● Bible References

"Him that cometh to me I will in no wise cast out."

(JOHN 6:37)

"If thou shalt confess . . . and believe in thine heart . . . thou shalt be saved."

(ROM. 10:9)

"Whosoever shall call upon the name of the Lord shall be saved."

(ROM. 10:13)

"Through his name . . . whosoever believeth in him shall receive remission of sins."

(ACTS 10:43)

"Come, let us reason together . . . though your sins be as scarlet, they shall be as white as snow."

(ISA. 1:18)

"Come unto me, all ye that labour and are heavy laden, and I will give you rest."

(MATT. 11:28)

"And I say unto you, Ask, and it shall be given unto you; seek, and ye shall find; knock, and it shall be opened unto you. For everyone that asketh receiveth."

(LUKE 11:9–10)

I've committed the unpardonable sin

This is often the most difficult problem to deal with since it is usually accompanied by emotional distress. Anyone who claims to have committed the unpardonable sin is hardly likely to have done so. If he had, he would have no feeling of concern over his soul's salvation and would manifest no desire to be forgiven. A person with this problem usually has deep emotional difficulties stemming from past relationships with parents or peers, and this restricts spiritual understanding. A person who lacked love in childhood tends to project his fears, guilts, and hurts on God. He may imagine God as unloving and uncaring like the people in his past. Nine times out of ten, therefore, this problem is psychological rather than spiritual. The Word of God is quick and sharp and powerful (Heb. 4:12). Use it to break through psychological barriers and bring about spiritual understanding. Explain that the unpardonable sin (Matt. 12:22–32) is a calculated resistance to God's Holy Spirit in which a person refuses to believe what deep in his heart he knows to be true. It is not something that happens in a moment but is a consistent and continued revolt against truth, light and holiness, similar to the rebellion of the angels who cannot receive forgiveness or salvation. Keep using scriptures in the face of all argument. Patient and prayerful counseling will often bring about a solution to this problem.

11

● Bible References

"God so loved the world, that he gave his Son."
(JOHN 3:16)

"No man is justified by the law in the sight of God. . . ."
(GAL. 3:11)

"Thou shalt love the Lord thy God with all thy heart, and with all thy soul, and with all thy mind."
(MATT. 22:37)

"But without faith it is impossible to please God."
(HEB. 11:6)

"He that believeth on the Son hath everlasting life."
(JOHN 3:36)

"Except your righteousness exceed that of the . . . Pharisees, ye shall in no case enter the kingdom of heaven."
(MATT. 5:20)

"By the deeds of the law there shall be no flesh justified in his sight."
(ROM. 3:20)

I do my best

Many rest their hope of eternal salvation on the false foundation of doing their best. The way to undermine this position is to show the person from Matthew 22:34–40 the standard which God has set for all men and women in His universe. Ask the person if he has kept this commandment. When he admits to having broken it, show him from James 2:10 that having broken one commandment, he is as guilty before God as if he had broken them all. Point out also that if doing one's best is all that is necessary to get to heaven, then God made a mistake in sending His Son to this earth to die upon a cross. Use this story to illustrate the point. A Christian when witnessing to a barber one day received this reply: "I am doing my best—surely God will accept that." The Christian said nothing. When the barber had finished cutting his hair, he rose from the chair and offered to help the barber cut the hair of his waiting customers. "But you can't do that," protested the barber; "you have not been trained." "But I will do my best," said the Christian. "Your best is not good enough," replied the barber. "No," said the Christian, "and neither is your best good enough for God." Point out that Christianity is different from every other religion in the world. Other religions try to climb the ladder that leads up to God, but the ladder is too high. They can never climb up to God. Christianity shows that God has come down the ladder. The Son of God became the Son of Man in order that the sons of men might become the sons of God.

12

Suggestions to adopt

WHEN DEALING WITH THE UNCONVERTED

- Depend on the Holy Spirit, not your argument, to illuminate people's minds.

- Don't be too *intense* in your approach. This puts people off.

- Listen carefully to what the other person has to say.

- Ask yourself: "Why is this question bothering him?" It will help you uncover the root cause underlying the question.

- Differentiate between the person and the problem. Don't allow any difficulty you may have in convincing the person of Christ's claims, to interfere with your respect for them as persons.

- Keep using the Bible as your authority. There is an awesome power in biblical texts when used.

- Don't be afraid to admit when you have no answer. Tell the person you will *find* the answer.

- Keep refocussing the issue onto Jesus Christ. Other issues can become vague but *He* is always clear.

THE following section deals with sixteen problems which are often raised by Christians and contains suggestions on how to deal with these difficulties, together with scripture references that relate to the particular situation. You will soon discover that as you begin to use these simple suggestions, you will be able to expand on them and build up additional insights and scripture references. Remember always to pray with a brother or sister who is in difficulty: this will help more than you could ever imagine.

Although at one time the major responsibility for counseling and helping Christians with their spiritual problems rested upon ministers and members of the clergy, something of a revolution is at present taking place within the Body of Christ as believers are beginning to see the truth of *every member ministry*.

More and more Christians are realizing that *every Christian* has a ministry within the Body of Christ, and part of that ministry is to encourage and support each other in times of personal trouble or difficulty. "God has put together the body in such a way that extra honor and care is given to those parts that might otherwise seem less important. This makes for happiness among the parts, so that the parts have the same care for each other that they do for themselves. If one part suffers, all parts suffer with it, and if one part is honored, all parts are glad" (1 Cor. 12:24–26, TLB).

Christian problems

● Bible References

"Whatsoever things are true, whatsoever things are honest . . . just . . . pure . . . lovely . . . good report. . . ."

(PHIL. 4:8)

"Set your affection on things above, not on things on the earth."

(COL. 3:2)

"Unto the pure all things are pure."

(TITUS 1:15)

"Let this mind be in you, which was in Christ. . . ."

(PHIL. 2:5)

"Whose mind is stayed on thee: because he trusteth in thee."

(ISA. 26:3)

"Stand in awe, and sin not: commune with your own heart. . . ."

(PS. 4:4)

"Meditate upon these things; give thyself wholly to them."

(1 TIM. 4:15)

Troubled by wrong thoughts

Be careful to point out to this person that wrong thoughts entering our minds are not in themselves sin. "We can't stop the birds from flying over our heads," said Martin Luther, "but we can stop them from building nests in our hair." Evil thoughts become sin only when the mind fondles them, nurtures them and continues to hold on to them. Encourage the concerned person not to repress the thoughts—that is, push them down into the subconscious—but to lift them up to God in praise. Though, at first, this might sound like a very unspiritual technique, explain to him how it works. When we push wrong thoughts into our subconscious mind and try to bury them there, these thoughts are not buried dead; they are buried *alive*. They continue to work in the subconscious. The best way to deal with wrong thoughts is to lift them up to God in an attitude of praise. Look how this principle works in the life of a Christian familiar with the technique. When a wrong thought enters his mind, he brings that wrong thought to God in an attitude of praise. He says: "Thank you, Lord, that this wrong thought draws my attention to you; it has become a steppingstone which is making me more aware of your presence in my life." Also encourage the person to spend a little time in reading the Scriptures when wrong thoughts come. Then these thoughts become an occasion to deepen one's fellowship with the Lord.

● Bible References

"When my heart is overwhelmed . . . lead me to the rock that is higher than I."

(PS. 61:2)

"For consider him that endured such contradiction of sinners. . . ."

(HEB. 12:3)

"Men ought always to pray, and not to faint."
(LUKE 18:1)

"When the enemy shall come in like a flood, the Spirit of the Lord shall lift up. . . ."

(ISA. 59:19)

"Casting all your care upon him; for he careth for you."

(1 PET. 5:7)

"Even when we are too weak to have any faith left, he remains faithful to us."
(2 TIM. 2:13, TLB)

"He hath said, I will never leave thee, nor forsake thee."

(HEB. 13:5b)

Easily upset

A person with this problem needs to be shown that it does not matter so much what happens to us, but how we react that is important. Share the truth which is found in James 1:2–3 (Phillips) and point out that according to these verses, there are two ways we can choose in responding to our problems: (1) resent them as intruders, or (2) welcome them as friends. We respond to trials and difficulties either with resentment and say, "Why should this happen to me?" or with praise and say, "God is sovereign. He will allow nothing to take place in my life unless He sees that it can be worked to good. I will accept this problem as a friend, put out the 'Welcome' mat, and watch what God will do." When we learn to accept life's problems with praise, we become free in our spirits to be creatively objective, enabling us to use problems for the development of our character and the improvement of our personalities. Point out to the person that according to Romans 8:28–29, God screens every event that takes place in our lives and permits only what He can use. If we respond to life's situations with gratitude rather than a grudge, we enable God by our cooperation to achieve His highest purpose in us, which is using the problems and irritations that beset us to shape our lives more closely to the image of His Son. People become upset when they fail to see their lives from God's point of view. Your task as a counselor here is to help them see their difficulties as tools in God's hands producing greater character and Christlikeness.

● Bible References

"Study to show thyself approved unto God, a workman. . . ."

(2 TIM. 2:15)

"And beside this, giving all diligence, add to your faith virtue; and to virtue knowledge."

(2 PET. 1:5)

"God has given each of us the ability to do certain things well."

(ROM. 12:6, TLB)

"Always keep your conscience clear. . . ."

(1 TIM. 1:19, TLB)

"If we confess our sins, he is faithful and just to forgive us our sins, and to cleanse us from all unrighteousness."

(1 JOHN 1:9)

"Thy word have I hid in mine heart, that I might not sin against thee."

(PS. 119:11)

"Put on the new man, which after God is created in righteousness and true holiness."

(EPH. 4:24)

Not growing spiritually

There are four major reasons why Christians fail to grow. You will need to cover them one by one as follows: (1) *Failure to maintain a clear conscience.* If any violation of God's Word is not dealt with immediately, this sin lies in the heart and festers. Probe gently to see if the person can remember violating God's Word in any way. Once discovered, begin to put it right. (2) *Neglect of personal prayer.* Every Christian needs to spend some time alone with God every day. If this Quiet Time is neglected, it will not be long before spiritual dryness sets in. Ask the person whether or not he or she has a daily appointment with God in prayer. (3) *Lack of daily Bible reading.* In order to grow, a Christian must have a daily intake from the Word of God, the Bible. The Word of God is a Christian's nourishment. Failure to feed one's spirit with the truths that flow out of Scripture will result in spiritual apathy and indifference. (4) *No clear understanding of one's place in the Body of Christ.** Many Christians become frustrated and fail to grow because they have never discovered their place in the Body of Christ. Every Christian is designed by God to fit into a special place in His Body, the Church. Examine Romans 12:6–8 to see the seven spiritual gifts which contribute to the growth and health of Christ's Body. *Every* Christian has at least one gift. Help the person discover and develop his gift.

---

*For a fuller explanation of this point, see *Discovering Your Place in the Body of Christ* by Selwyn Hughes.

● Bible References

"Be honest in your estimate of yourselves, measuring your value by how much faith God has given you."

(ROM. 12:3, TLB)

"God has given us the ability to do certain things well."

(ROM. 12:6)

"You saw me before I was born, and scheduled each day of my life before I began to breathe."

(PS. 139:16, TLB)

"Man looketh on the outward appearance, but the Lord looketh on the heart."

(1 SAM. 16:7)

"Knowing what lies ahead for you, you won't become bored with being a Christian, nor become spiritually dull and indifferent."

(HEB. 6:12, TLB)

"Having predestinated us unto the adoption of children by Jesus Christ to himself, according to the good pleasure of his will. . . ."

(EPH. 1:5)

"Now unto him that is able to do exceeding abundantly above all we ask or think, according to the power that worketh in us. . . ."

(EPH. 3:20)

Inferiority complex

Our image of ourselves is constructed from the opinions reflected to us by parents, friends, and relatives in the early years of our development. A child who feels deeply loved will grow up with a healthy sense of self-worth. A child who is rejected and treated with disrespect will grow up with feelings of deep inferiority. Such a person should be encouraged to view himself through God's eyes. Share with him John 1:42, "Thou art Simon [Greek: a piece of rock] but thou shalt be . . . Cephas [Greek: a rock]." There were three Simon Peters: (1) The one his friends saw; (2) the one he himself saw; (3) the one Christ saw. Others saw in Peter something small and insignificant (a piece of rock), but Jesus saw in him something strong and secure (a rock). Christ sees us not as we are, but as we can become by His power. Encourage this person to ask himself, "How does God see me now that I am a Christian?" Help him to answer this by sharing the scriptures listed. You can also challenge the person concerned by asking: "Who is the real you? Is it the person you yourself see? Is it the person your friends see? Is it the person God sees?" The real self is the person God *means* you to be. Focus on that, dwell upon it daily in prayer, and the ideal will turn into the actual.

● Bible References

"For our light affliction, which is but for a moment. . . ."

(2 COR. 4:17)

"Why art thou cast down, O my soul?"

(PS. 42:5)

"In God I will praise his word, in God I have put my trust. . . ."

(PS. 56:4)

"And we know that all things work together for good to them that love God."

(ROM. 8:28)

"Bow down thine ear to me; deliver me speedily . . . be thou my strong rock for an house of defence to save me."

(PS. 31:2)

"When thou passest through the waters, I will be with thee; and through the rivers, they shall not overflow thee."

(ISA. 43:2)

"The Lord is close to those whose hearts are breaking."

(PS. 34:18, TLB)

Depression

Depression should never be viewed lightly. Avoid saying to a depressed person "Cheer up" or "Snap out of it." Such statements are not helpful but, in fact, prove counter-productive. Share with the person some insights from the way God treated Elijah's depression in 1 Kings 19. First, God made sure that Elijah had enough sleep and enough to eat. Lack of sleep and an improper diet are often contributory causes of depression. Second, God waited until Elijah was well rested before He confronted him with the question, "What doest thou here?" Make sure the person has had enough food and rest before attempting to explore basic causes. Third, God encouraged Elijah to talk about his problem and ventilate his feelings. Be a good listener and encourage the person to share with you what he considers is the basic cause of his depression. Fourth, God gave Elijah a special task to complete for Him. A depressed person needs to become involved in doing something for others, for in this way he breaks the vicious circle of self-centeredness which is often a basic cause of his emotional problems. In a case of serious depression where the person is unable to cope with the ordinary, routine duties of life, a medical checkup is advisable. Some forms of depression are chemically based and are greatly helped by proper medication.

5

● Bible References

"These trials are only to test your faith, to see whether or not it is strong and pure."

(1 PET. 1:7, TLB)

"Everything that has happened to me here has been a great boost in getting out the Good News concerning Christ."

(PHIL. 1:12, TLB)

"The Lord bringeth the counsel of the heathen to nought: he maketh the devices of the people of none effect."

(PS. 33:10)

"As far as I am concerned God turned into good what you meant for evil."

(GEN. 50:20, TLB)

"Even when we are too weak to have any faith left, he remains faithful to us."

(2 TIM. 2:13, TLB)

"Take therefore no thought for the morrow: for the morrow shall take thought for the things of itself."

(MATT. 6:34)

"And now just as you trusted Christ to save you, trust him, too, for each day's problems; live in vital union with him."

(COL. 2:6, TLB)

Feelings of failure

In some way and at some time everyone experiences failure. However, this factor is of little help to someone who may have failed an important examination or a special project. First, work with the person in attempting to discover the cause of the failure. Was it unwise planning, failure to anticipate, attempting something beyond his ability, failing to work hard enough, following wrong advice, etc.? An honest look at the causes will prevent the seeds of failure taking root. Second, get the person to admit that he has failed. If not honestly faced, it will become repressed and cause further problems at a later stage. Encourage him to see the overruling providence of God as illustrated in Romans 8:28. Show that God is not helpless in the face of failure, but can turn everything harmful that happens to us, to good. If after this advice the person still has deep feelings of failure, suggest a medical checkup. A Christian doctor says, "Little by little the human body can become adjusted to feeling below par. Finally you can reach the point where you are really not physically able to handle things the way you should. This can lead to many types of failure in life."

6

● Bible References

"Let not sin, therefore, reign in your mortal body, that ye should obey it in the lusts thereof."

(ROM. 6:12)

"For sin shall not have dominion over you, for you are not under law but under grace."

(ROM. 6:14)

"Every man is tempted when he is drawn away of his own lust and enticed."

(JAMES 1:14)

"If any man come after me, let him deny himself, and take up his cross, and follow me."

(MATT. 16:24)

"Away then with sinful, earthly things: deaden the evil desires lurking within you; have nothing to do with sexual sin, impurity, lust and shameful desires."

(COL. 3:5, TLB)

"Don't fool yourselves. Those who live immoral lives, who are idol worshippers, adulterers, or homosexuals—will have no share in his kingdom. . . . There was a time when some of you were like that but now your sins are washed away."

(1 COR. 6:9, 11, TLB)

Homosexual tendencies

Homosexual tendencies consist of a sexual attraction for a person of the same sex, and the practice of homosexuality is strongly denounced in the Bible (Gen. 18:20, 19:5; Lev. 20:13). Although a homosexual person may feel an inclination toward a person of the same sex, the inclination in itself is not sin. It becomes sin when it is encouraged by fantasizing, or expresses itself in a definite act. Encourage the person to bring about a change in his thought and behavior patterns through meditation in the Scriptures. Where a definite act of homosexuality has been committed, take the person through the following steps: (1) Recognize it as a sin. (2) Repent of it, asking God's forgiveness. (3) Reconstruct the thought life by meditation in the Word of God. Some feel that homosexual tendencies can't be cured. In recent years, however, a growing number of Christians have found freedom from this problem by focusing on carefully selected passages of scripture and meditating on them. The constant washing of their thoughts by scripture has gradually eliminated their homosexual tendencies. Basically, all psychological and spiritual problems stem from wrong thinking. The more a person trains himself to think as God thinks, through scripture meditation, the greater the possibility of producing right personality development.

7

● Bible References

"But be filled with the Spirit. . . . Wives submit yourselves unto your own husbands. . . . Husbands love your wives."

(EPH. 5:18–25)

"Be patient with each other, making allowance for each other's faults because of your love. . . ."

(EPH. 4:2, TLB)

"Be humble, thinking of others as better than yourself."

(PHIL. 2:3, TLB)

"Wives, submit yourselves unto your own husbands. Husbands, love your wives, and be not bitter against them. . . ."

(COL. 3:18–19)

"Give, and it shall be given unto you; good measure, pressed down, and shaken together, and running over."

(LUKE 6:38)

"You husbands must be careful of your wives, being thoughtful of their needs and honoring them as the weaker sex."

(1 PET. 3:7, TLB)

Marriage is breaking up

There are about twenty to thirty specific reasons why marriages break apart, and many of these reasons can be narrowed down to one basic reason—*self-centeredness*. This comes about when one person is more concerned about getting his own needs met than in meeting the needs of his partner. In marriage we can be either a *giver* or a *getter*. Givers delight to meet the needs of their partner, while getters are more concerned about having their own needs met. No real progress can be made in dealing with the other problems that arise in marriage unless this is solved. Encourage the person to ask himself this basic question: "Am I more concerned in meeting the needs of my partner than I am in having my own needs met?" Show him that Christ's love can, if allowed, sweep into his life and shift him from being a self-centered person to a Christ-centered one. Those who are self-centered are "getters," while Christ-centered persons are "givers." Use the scriptures listed to drive this point home. It is important also to point out that the most basic need a man has in his life is the need for *significance*, while a woman's most basic need is *security*. When a man sets out in his marriage to make his wife feel secure by ministering to her needs, the woman in turn ministers to her husband's need for significance. In giving of themselves to each other, they will discover fulfillment and joy.

8

● Bible References

"Heaviness in the heart of man maketh it stoop: but a good word maketh it glad."

(PROV. 12:25)

"A sound heart is the life of the flesh, but envy the rottenness of the bones."

(PROV. 14:30)

"A merry heart doeth good like a medicine. . . ."

(PROV. 17:22)

"Which of you by taking thought can add one cubit unto his stature?"

(MATT. 6:27)

"Be careful for nothing, but in everything by prayer and supplication. . . ."

(PHIL. 4:6–7)

"Casting all your care upon him: for he careth for you."

(1 PET. 5:7)

"Look at the birds! They don't worry about what to eat . . . for your heavenly father feeds them. And you are far more valuable to him than they are."

(MATT. 6:26, TLB)

Worry

The basic cause of most worry and anxiety is a failure to handle life on a day-to-day basis. God means us to live our lives a day at a time. Though, of course, it is wise and prudent to plan for the future, we are not to worry about it (Matt. 6:31–34). This person will need to be taken to Romans 8:28 and shown that God is in control of all situations, and when human plans are crossed and thwarted, God is able to turn every stumbling block into a steppingstone. Encourage the person to put all his energy into living a day at a time, as using energy to try to cope with what *might* happen tomorrow is self-defeating. Use the three simple steps below to help him see things in perspective. (1) *What is my problem?* Get him to write this down on a sheet of paper. (2) *What does God want me to do about this problem?* Help him to identify clearly what steps God expects him to take in relation to the problem. Pray with him at this stage. (3) *When, where, and how should I begin?* Plan a simple course of action and encourage him to believe that when he does the *possible*, God will do the *impossible*. Someone asked a Christian how he managed to keep free from worry. He replied: "I know that God won't let anything come my way that He and I together can't handle." Share this simple truth also with the person concerned. It has helped thousands of others. It may well help him.

9

● Bible References

"Cast thy burden upon the Lord, and he shall sustain thee."

(PS. 55:22)

"Let not your heart be troubled: ye believe in God, believe also in me."

(JOHN 14:1)

"He will swallow up death in victory: and the Lord will wipe away tears from off all faces."

(ISA. 25:8)

"He will be very gracious unto thee at the voice of thy cry."

(ISA. 30:19)

"O death, where is thy sting? O grave, where is thy victory?"

(1 COR. 15:55)

"Blessed are they that mourn: for they shall be comforted."

(MATT. 5:4)

"Blessed is the Lord, for he has shown me that his never-failing love protects me like the walls of a fort!"

(PS. 31:21, TLB)

Lost a loved one

Even when death comes to a loved one after a long illness, grief is still a hard burden to bear. Encourage the bereaved person to talk, as he needs to talk out his inner feelings more than to hear comments or advice. Overcome any reluctance he might have to remain silent by gently and lovingly probing him with questions. At an appropriate moment (and if the deceased was a Christian) explain that the Bible pictures death as great gain for the believer. Share some of the reasons why a Christian is happy in heaven (Rev. 21:3–4). If the deceased was not a Christian, discuss some of the positive qualities which he or she possessed. This is being supportive, without going further than God's Word and suggesting that there is hope when there is none. Pray with the person concerned and attempt to verbalize his feelings, bringing out into the open buried thoughts and feelings, such as "Why did this happen?" and "How can I bear such a loss?" Offer help in a practical way as grief temporarily paralyzes routine activities. Be alert for things needing immediate attention. In attempting to be a comforter to someone who has lost a loved one, be sincere and honest. If you do not really understand the person's problem, admit it. Letting the person know that you *care* may be the help he needs.

10

● Bible References

"Learn to put aside your own desires. . . . This will make possible the next step, which is for you to enjoy other people, and to like them, and finally you will grow to love them deeply."

(2 PET. 1:6–7, TLB)

"When a man's ways please the Lord, he maketh even his enemies to be at peace with him."

(PROV. 16:7)

"Love forgets mistakes; nagging about them parts the best of friends."

(PROV. 17:9, TLB)

"For the Holy Spirit, God's gift, does not want you to be afraid of people, but to be wise and strong, and to love them and enjoy being with them."

(2 TIM. 1:7, TLB)

"Now you can have real love for everyone because your souls have been cleansed from selfishness and hatred when you trusted Christ to save you."

(1 PET. 1:22, TLB)

"A true friend is always loyal, and a brother is born to help in time of need."

(PROV. 17:17, TLB)

Difficulty making friends

The main reason why people have difficulty in making friends is due to the fact that they have never truly accepted themselves. If we do not accept ourselves, we will have trouble in accepting others, and this negative attitude will be reflected in our relationships. Encourage the person to see himself as God sees him, *in Christ*, a person of immense significance and worth. Tell him, "There never was and never will be another you. You are unique in all the universe." Once a person discovers his true identity in Christ, his ability to relate to others is greatly improved, as he no longer compares himself to other people but to Christ. Share with him the importance of looking at everyone he meets through Christ's eyes, asking himself two basic questions: "What is God doing in this person's life? How can I cooperate with Him?" This attitude will change the focus from "How can I *get* a friend?" to "How can I *be* a friend?" Someone once said: "To have a friend, be friendly." Share also the five important principles of building friendships: (1) Be alert to each new person around you. (2) Develop a cheerful countenance. (3) Learn to greet people by name. (4) Ask appropriate questions. (5) Be a good listener.

11

● Bible References

"If my people, which are called by my name, shall humble themselves, and pray. . . ."
(2 CHRON. 7:14)

"I exhort therefore that . . . supplications, prayers, intercessions. . . ."
(1 TIM. 2:1)

"Pray without ceasing. In everything give thanks."
(1 THESS. 5:17–18)

"In everything by prayer and supplication with thanksgiving. . . ."
(PHIL. 4:6)

"When thou prayest, enter thy closet . . . pray to thy Father."
(MATT. 6:6)

"For the Lord is watching his children, listening to their prayers."
(1 Pet. 3:12, TLB)

"Ask, and it shall be given you; seek, and ye shall find; knock, and it shall be opened unto you."
(LUKE 11:9)

Hard to pray

Offer this person the following suggestions and encourage him to put them into operation immediately: (1) *Make a daily prayer appointment with God and keep it.* In earthly affairs when we make an appointment with someone, we keep that appointment whether we feel like it or not. Making a daily appointment with God means that courtesy will carry us into His presence even if feeling doesn't. (2) *Begin your prayer time by meditating in the Scriptures.* Experience has shown that the best way to begin one's daily prayer is by meditating on a passage from the Bible. This devotional meditation prepares the soul in a wonderful way for fellowship and communion with the Lord. (3) *Use a prayer list.* Put down on a piece of paper items about which you want to pray, and talk to God about them. (4) *Pray out loud, if possible.* Hearing ourselves pray often gives a deeper intensity to prayer. (5) *Don't fight wandering thoughts—use them.* Encourage the person to pray for the thing to which his mind wanders. In this way he can weave even wandering thoughts into the pattern of his prayers. (6) *Thank God for what He has done for you.* God wants us to be thankful. Think on all He has done, and the heart will soon begin to swell with gratitude.

12

● Bible References

"Therefore being justified by faith, we have peace with God. . . ."

(ROM. 5:11)

"But as many as received him, to them gave he power to become the sons of God. . . ."

(JOHN 1:12)

"The Spirit itself beareth witness with our spirit, that we are the children of God."

(ROM. 8:16)

"We know we have passed from death unto life, because we love the brethren. . . ."

(1 JOHN 3:14)

"If any man be in Christ, he is a new creature. . . ."

(2 COR. 5:17)

"God is not a man that he should lie. . . ."

(NUM. 23:19)

"Ye have received the Spirit of adoption, whereby we cry, Abba, Father."

(ROM. 8:15)

Doubts about salvation

A person who has this problem needs to be encouraged to share his understanding of what "salvation" really means. He may never have understood what it means to be "saved" and might require the way of salvation explained to him in a clear manner. If, however, he has a clear grasp of its meaning, and has apparently received Christ but lacks assurance, then proceed by asking him the following questions: (1) *When you accepted Christ, did you allow Him to take up the center of your life, or did you relegate Him to a marginal part of your being?* Christ is not able to give assurance unless He has been admitted to the central part of one's life. He must be *Lord* as well as Savior. (2) *When you decided for Christ, did you repent of your sin, or were you just sorry for the consequences?* Some attempt to become Christians without showing sorrow for keeping God out of their spirits—the part He made for himself. (3) *Are you holding feelings of bitterness against anyone who has wronged you?* This is often a cause for lack of assurance, as the person is unable to feel the full effect of God's forgiveness until he releases any unforgiveness he holds in his heart toward another.

13

67

● Bible References

"The blood of Jesus Christ his Son cleanses us from all sin."

(1 JOHN 1:7)

"If we confess our sins, he is faithful and just to forgive us our sins. . . ."

(1 JOHN 1:9)

"Let the wicked forsake his way . . . and let him return unto the Lord, and he will have mercy upon him. . . ."

(ISA. 55:7)

"In whom we have . . . the forgiveness of sins, according to the riches of his grace."

(EPH. 1:7)

"For thou, Lord, art ready to forgive, and plenteous in mercy. . . ."

(PS. 86:5)

"It was through what his Son did that God cleared a path for everything to come to him. . . . For Christ's death on the cross has made peace with God for all by his blood."

(COL. 1:20, TLB)

"Brothers! Listen! In this man Jesus, there is forgiveness for your sins! Everyone who trusts in him is freed from guilt and declared righteous.

(ACTS 13:38–39, TLB)

Committed terrible sin

Begin by reading the passage in 1 John 1:9 and explain that providing we take the right steps concerning our sin and adopt the right attitude toward it, then there is no sin that cannot be forgiven. This does not mean that God delights in our sin. He is hurt—deeply hurt—when we violate His laws, but so great is His love that He has provided in the shed blood of the Lord Jesus Christ a way by which our sin can be covered and forgiven. Share with the person the following steps: (1) *Confession*. Encourage a full confession in which nothing is held back. Get him to identify the sin by naming it so that he can see it as it really is. (2) *Repentance*. Repentance is not simply being sorry for sin, but being sorry for the deep self-centered attitude that led to it being committed. It is this that must be repented of. (3) *Ask God to forgive, and at the same time receive His forgiveness*. Encourage the person not only to ask but also to accept the forgiveness of God by saying, "I receive your forgiveness through Jesus Christ, my Lord." (4) *Take a fresh grip upon God*. Help the person to rededicate himself to God and to His service. (5) *Make restitution if necessary*. If the sin has harmed anyone else, then encourage the person to ask forgiveness of the one who has been hurt. Make sure the person understands the need to put right (as far as is humanly possible) any wrong that has been done.

14

● Bible References

"It is his glory to pass over a transgression."
(PROV. 19:11)

"Forbearing one another and forgiving one another...."
(COL. 3:13)

"Recompense to no man evil for evil...."
(ROM. 12:17)

"Be kind to one another, tenderhearted, forgiving one another...."
(EPH. 4:32)

"If thy brother trespass against thee, rebuke him: ... if he repent, forgive him."
(LUKE 17:3)

"See that none render evil for evil unto any man, but ever follow that which is good...."
(1 THESS. 5:15)

"Your heavenly father will forgive you if you forgive those who sin against you, but if you refuse to forgive them, he will not forgive you."
(MATT. 6:14–15, TLB)

Difficult to forgive

The desire to hold bitterness and resentment against someone who has injured us lies deep in the human heart. Unforgiveness, however, has serious spiritual and psychological consequences. Explain to the person concerned that forgiveness involves two things: (1) *wiping the slate clean in relation to the offense*, and (2) *handing over to God the responsibility for discipline or punishment.* It is important to make this clear, as some people say they are willing to forgive but not to forget. Next, get the person to make a list of the hurts and offenses which need to be forgiven. This ensures that nothing remains hidden to come up at another time. Then encourage the person to view these hurts and offenses from God's point of view. Show him that God has been using hurts to improve his character, as the offenses and injuries suffered by us become, in God's hands, the best "teachers" for developing our characters and spiritual effectiveness. Next, get him to reflect on what God has done for him: as we see the depth of God's forgiveness in our lives, it motivates us toward forgiveness of others. Finally, show him that forgiveness is an act of the will. If we wait until we feel like forgiving, we may never do it. We must obey the command of Ephesians 4:32 and say, by an act of the will, "I forgive this person in Jesus' Name, just as Christ has forgiven me."

15

● Bible References

"This poor man cried, and the Lord heard him, and saved him out of all his troubles. . . ."

(PS. 34:6)

"We are perplexed because we don't know why things happen to us as they do, but we don't give up. We get knocked down, but we get up again and keep going."

(2 COR. 4:8–9, TLB)

"God will not allow you to be tested beyond your power to remain firm: at the time you are put to the test, he will give you the strength to endure it, and so provide you with a way out. . . ."

(1 COR. 10:13, Good News Bible)

"Let us therefore come boldly to the throne of grace, that we may obtain mercy and find grace to help in time of need."

(HEB. 4:16)

"Even when we are too weary to have any faith left, he remains faithful to us, and will help us, for he cannot disown us, who are part of himself."

(2 TIM. 2:13, TLB)

Contemplating suicide

When confronted by this statement, the first thing you should do is to *communicate your personal interest* by letting the person know how glad you are that he shared this information with you. Be a good listener and encourage him to talk over the problem with you. Be sure not to challenge or criticize anything he says, or make any value judgments on his behavior at this stage. Try to clarify the basic problem as quickly as possible. Say something like this: "I'm interested in knowing what it is that has brought you to these conclusions. Would you like to share them with me?" Concentrate on piecing together the bits of information you receive from the distressed person, in order to put the whole problem into perspective. When you have clarified what the problem is, then share with the person concerned a sense of hope that you will personally assist in helping him solve the problem. The cardinal rules of helping those who are suicidal are these: (1) *Activity:* The person needs to feel something is being done. (2) *Authority:* The person needs to feel you are able to take charge. (3) *Involvement:* The person needs to feel that you will take a personal interest in the solution of his problem.

Turn to next page for further instructions on how to handle suicidal cases.

16

Do's and don'ts

IN RELATION TO THE SUICIDAL

Do take seriously every suicidal threat, comment, or act. Suicide is no joke. Don't be afraid to ask the person if he is really thinking about committing suicide. The mention won't plant the idea in his head. Rather, it will relieve him to know that he is being taken seriously, that he is better understood than he suspected.

DON'T dismiss a suicidal threat and underestimate its importance. Never say, "Oh, forget it. You won't kill yourself. You can't really mean it. You're not the type." That kind of remark may be a challenge to a suicidal person. Such a person needs attention, not dismissal. Anyone desperate enough can be "the type."

DON'T try to shock or challenge the person by saying, "Oh, go ahead and do it." Such an impatient remark may be hard to hold back if a person has been repeating his threats or has been bothersome to have around. But it is a careless invitation to suicide.

DON'T try to analyze the person's behavior and confront him with interpretations of his actions and feelings during the moment of crisis. That should be done later by a professional.

DON'T argue with the individual about whether he should live or die. That argument can't be won. The only possible position to take is that the person MUST live.

DON'T assume that time heals all wounds and everything will get better by itself. That can happen, but it can't be counted on.

DO be willing to listen. You may have heard the story before, but hear it again. Be genuinely interested, be strong, stable, and firm. Promise the person that everything possible will be done to keep him alive, because that is what he needs most.*

---

*Published by the Public Affairs Committee in New York.

THE following section deals with the intellectual excuses which thinking and thoughtful people give as reasons for rejecting Christ and the truth of Christianity. It is important to see these for what they are—"excuses," and not genuine problems. Josh McDowell, an evangelist who has been deeply involved in dealing with university and college students, and has ministered in over 400 universities, in 42 countries, says, "I have met many men with intellectual excuses, but few with intellectual problems."

The truth is that most people (not all) who advance intellectual arguments as to why they reject Christianity do so, not because they have a genuine intellectual problem, but because they are unprepared and unwilling to submit their wills to Jesus Christ, and to have their lifestyle radically changed.

Mainly, there are four basic reasons why people reject Christianity:

1. **Ignorance.** These are the people who have never read the Bible or heard the way of salvation. In many cases this ignorance, however, is self-imposed, as deep in their hearts they are aware of their moral accountability to God, but they keep their distance from anything religious in an attempt to use ignorance as a final excuse for rejecting the God that nature and their conscience tells them exists (Rom. 1:18–20).

2. **Pride.** These are the people who struggle to maintain an egocentric and self-centered position in the midst of their own universe, and will not admit that they need God's help in obtaining eternal salvation (John 5:40–44).

3. **Bitterness.** These claim that there is so much suffering and injustice in the world that God cannot possibly be interested in the affairs of the inhabitants of the earth. "If He is not concerned with us," they claim, "why should we be concerned with Him?"
4. **Moral impurity.** These are so caught up in sensuality and the pleasures of the flesh that they are unwilling to give up their present lifestyle. They resent the fact that God will demand an inward change and thus they choose to reject Him.

It is often true that people reject Christ not because of problems in their minds but because of a problem with their will. It is not so much "I can't" but "I won't." A counselor when discussing an intellectual excuse with a brilliant young university student said, "If I can prove to your satisfaction the claim of Christianity to be true, will you then receive Christ?" Her reply was no. He said, "Then your problem is not in your mind, but in your will." It is important in dealing with non-Christians to point out whenever they refuse to accept the argument for Christianity that their problem might not be intellectual (in the mind) but volitional (in the will).

Paul Little has pointed out that every Christian has a responsibility to try to answer the intellectual arguments of thoughtful and thinking people. He claims that there are two wrong positions that Christians can adopt in relation to this matter:
1. An anti-intellectual attitude in which they withdraw from all discussion at an intellectual level.

2. A pro-intellectual attitude in which they think that all that is necessary is skillful argument and reasoned debate.

John Stott has said that "while we must not pander to a man's intellectual arrogance, we must cater to his intellectual integrity." We owe it to thinking men and women to give "a reason for the hope that is within us."

On the other hand, we must not overemphasize this and go to the other extreme. People are won to Christ not by human argument (that helps) but by the regenerating power of the Holy Spirit. There must always be complete and utter dependency upon Him, for "no man can say that 'Jesus is Lord' and really mean it unless the Holy Spirit is helping him" (1 Cor. 12:3, TLB).

Some years ago a group of Christians working with university students were impressed by the fact that in their discussions with young intellectuals, certain questions kept recurring. They discovered that eight basic questions kept coming up time after time in discussion. These eight questions, together with counseling suggestions, form the next section of this booklet. Acquainting yourself with these questions will help you in your task of dealing with those who offer intellectual excuses.

Intellectual excuses

● Bible References

"And there came a voice out of the cloud, saying, This is my beloved Son: hear him."

(LUKE 9:35)

"And the Word . . . dwelt among us . . . full of truth."

(JOHN 1:14)

"Truth came by Jesus Christ."

(JOHN 1:17)

"The true worshipper shall worship the Father in spirit and in truth, for the Father seeketh such."

(JOHN 4:23)

"Then said Jesus to those . . . which believe on him . . . Ye shall know the truth and the truth shall make you free."

(JOHN 8:31–32)

"Jesus said . . . No man cometh unto the Father but by me."

(JOHN 14:6)

"Neither is there salvation in any other: for there is none other name under heaven given among men, whereby we must be saved."

(ACTS 4:12)

Aren't all religions the same?

The inference behind this question is that adherents of other religions worship the same God as a Christian, only under a different name, so why should Christians insist that Jesus is the only way to God? The most important thing in life is truth. "Faith is no more valid," said someone, "than the object in which it is placed." If we want to get to heaven, then we owe it to ourselves to make sure that our faith is pinned on that which is true. As non-Christian religions differ from the Christian religion over the place given to Jesus Christ, and as Christ himself said that He is the only way to God, then the matter is crucial. Whom are we to believe? Christ himself or those who have framed the world's religions? There may be many paths by which we come to Jesus Christ, but Jesus Christ himself said that *He* is the only way by which we come to God. Do not be afraid of being regarded as bigoted when presenting the truth of the preeminence and indispensability of Christ. The issue is too critical as there is no other option apart from Christ. If you are going to be faithful to what Christ says, then take your stand firmly and positively on the truth of the Scripture that there is but one way to God and that way is through the person of God's Son, Jesus Christ himself.

● Bible References

*"God said unto Moses . . . Say . . . I AM hath
sent me unto you."*

(EX. 3:14)

---

*"Jesus said . . . I AM the bread of life . . . the
living bread which came down from heaven."*
(JOHN 6:35, 51)

---

*"Jesus saith . . . I AM the way, the truth, and
the life."*

(JOHN 14:6)

---

*"In the beginning was the Word, and the Word
was with God, and the Word was God. All things
were made by him. And the Word was made
flesh and dwelt among us."*

(JOHN 1:1, 3, 14)

"I and my Father are one."

(JOHN 10:30)

"He that hath seen me hath seen the Father."
(JOHN 14:9)

---

*"But unto the Son he saith, Thy throne, O God,
is forever and ever: a sceptre of righteousness is
the sceptre of thy kingdom."*

(HEB. 1:8)

Is Jesus Christ really God?

Someone has said that the "acid test of Christianity is Christ." In other words, Christianity rises and falls on the position we give to Jesus Christ. If Jesus Christ is not God, then He cannot possibly give salvation to men. The following scriptural arguments will help you disprove the theory that Jesus Christ is not God: (1) If Christ is not God, then He was wrong to accept the worship of Thomas (John 20:28), for worship given to a creature or a created being is idolatry. (2) If Jesus Christ is not God, then how is it that His most intimate friends came to believe and teach that He was? (3) If Jesus Christ is not God, then why does the Scripture give Him equal status with God in the creation of the universe? (Compare Gen. 1:1 and Col. 1:16.) (4) If Jesus Christ is not God, then how can He claim to forgive sins, seeing this right belongs to God alone? (Matt. 9:6). If Jesus Christ is not God, then why did He teach that all men should honor Him just as they should honor the Father? (See John 5:22–23.) In this passage it can be seen that Jesus presents a warning to those who accuse Him of blasphemy. He tells them that by hurling abuse at Him, they are actually hurling it at God, and God is offended by their treatment of His Son. It is quite clear from this that to dishonor Jesus is to dishonor God, for Jesus *is* God.

2

● Bible References

"He said . . . They that be whole need not a physician, but they that are sick . . . for I am not come to call the righteous, but sinners to repentance."

(MATT. 9:12–13)

"Wherefore I say unto thee, Her sins, which are many, are forgiven: for she loved much: but to whom little is forgiven, the same loveth little."

(LUKE 7:47)

"Not so many wise . . . not many mighty, not many noble are called. But God hath chosen the foolish . . . the weak . . . and base . . . and things which are not . . . that no flesh should glory in his presence."

(1 COR. 1:26–29)

"If any man be in Christ, he is a new creature: old things are passed away: behold, all things are become new."

(2 COR. 5:17)

"By the grace of God I am what I am."

(1 COR. 15:10)

" 'I don't know whether he is good or bad,' the man replied, 'but I know this: I was blind, and now I see.' "

(JOHN 9:25, TLB)

Can't Christianity be explained psychologically?

The inference behind this question is that Christians are the product of childhood conditioning and psychological pressures. The thought is sometimes advanced that people become Christians because of what they were taught in their childhood days and are merely responding to preconditioning. This is an oversimplification of the issue, as a good deal of evidence can be advanced to show that Christians come from every imaginable background, many being converted to Christ from an atheistic upbringing or an agnostic background. Another inference in this argument is that Christians become changed individuals through self-hypnosis; they hypnotize themselves into believing what they want to believe. Point out that it would be a new thing if hypnosis could make an immoral person pure, a thief honest, and a criminal straight. In the final analysis, no one can argue with experience—that's why a Christian's testimony to the changing power of Jesus Christ is so effective. Share the changes that have taken place in your own life since you came to know Jesus Christ. Three things should be emphasized: (1) the kind of life you lived prior to your conversion; (2) how you came to know Jesus Christ and accepted Him as your Lord and Savior; (3) specific results of the change He has made in your life since you came to know Him.

● Bible References

"There is no God else beside me; a just God and a Saviour; there is none beside me."

(ISA. 45:21)

"A just weight and balance are the Lord's: all the weights of the bag are his work."

(PROV. 16:11)

"Good and upright is the Lord, therefore he will teach sinners in the way."

(PS. 25:8)

"Lift up your eyes on high and behold who created these things."

(ISA. 40:26)

"The heavens declare the glory of God and the firmament showeth his handiwork."

(PS. 19:1)

"We may be sure that all this will be taken into account in the day of true judgment, when God will judge men's secret lives by Christ Jesus, as my gospel plainly states."

(ROM. 2:16, Phillips)

What about the heathen?

Although the Bible does not tell us in precise detail how God will deal with this class of people, there are a number of scriptural facts which enable us to come to some definite conclusions. (1) *God is just.* All the evidence of the Bible shows that God will always act in harmony with His character, which is just and good (Gen. 18:25). (2) The evidence of a Creator is seen in creation (Rom. 1:19–20). For those who want to see, the evidence of God's existence is clearly displayed in the material universe. (3) No person will be condemned for rejecting Jesus Christ, of whom he has never heard, but for the violation of his own moral standards (Rom. 2:12–16; John 1:4–5). (4) If a person responds to the light he has, and seeks God, then God will, in some way, enable him to hear of Jesus Christ (Jer. 29:13; Matt. 7:7–11). Sometimes a person will raise this question concerning the destiny of the heathen in order to divert attention away from any personal sense of conviction he may be feeling about the demands of Christianity. This fact needs to be presented to the person lovingly and gently. Terminate the discussion by focusing on this truth; God being just and righteous will bring all these things to a satisfactory conclusion. The important issue you should be thinking of at this moment is what *you* are going to do about the matter of *your* relationship with Jesus Christ.

● Bible References

"All scripture is given by inspiration of God and is profitable. . . ."

(2 TIM. 3:16)

"Holy men of God spake as they were moved by the Holy Spirit."

(2 PET. 1:21)

"Sanctify them through thy truth: thy word is truth."

(JOHN 17:17)

"Then said the Lord . . . I will hasten my word to perform it."

(JER. 1:12)

"Then shall ye know that I, the Lord, hath spoken it, and performed it, saith the Lord."

(EZEK. 37:14)

"O taste and see that the Lord is good. . . ."

(PS. 34:8)

"Did not our hearts glow within us while He was talking to us on the road, and opened the scriptures to us?"

(LUKE 24:32, Berkeley Version)

"The word of our God shall stand forever."

(ISA. 40:8)

The Bible is full of errors

Ask the person what particular error he has in mind. Nine times out of ten a person who makes this statement does so because he has heard someone else say that the Bible is full of contradictions. He has not gone on to do any research for himself. If the person is unable to come up with a specific example, do not engage in ridicule. Under no circumstances should you make fun of anyone or attempt to make them look foolish. This approach proves counter-productive. Share your personal testimony of how reliable and accurate you have found Christ's promise of peace, pardon and security in your own life. Point out that Jesus' promise, "My peace I give unto you" (John 14:27), is something you have proved personally since you came to know Him as your Lord and Savior. Think of other examples of promises Christ made which you have personally proved. If on the other hand, the person does come up with an apparent contradiction, and you don't have an immediate answer, do not panic. Smile, and say, "I don't have the answer to your question at the moment, but I'll be delighted to look it up and give you the answer later." The Bible does contain some apparent contradictions, but there are satisfactory answers to almost all of these issues. Almost any Christian bookshop will direct you to the books you ought to study which deal with the apparent contradictions of Scripture. *Difficulties in the Bible* by R. A. Torrey (Moody Press) is an excellent book to study on apparent contradictions.

● Bible References

"For thou wilt not leave my soul in hell; neither wilt thou suffer thine Holy One to see corruption."

(PS. 16:10)

"And the third day he shall rise again."
(MATT. 20:19)

"Ye seek Jesus of Nazareth, which was crucified: he is risen; he is not here."

(MARK 16:6)

"Afterwards he appeared unto the eleven as they sat at meat, and upbraided them with their unbelief . . . because they believed not them which had seen him after he was risen."

(MARK 16:14)

"For Christ also hath once suffered for sins, the just for the unjust, that he might bring us to God, being put to death in the flesh, but quickened by the Spirit."

(1 PET. 3:18)

"The Son of man must suffer many things, and be rejected of the elders and chief priests and scribes, and be slain, and be raised the third day."

(LUKE 9:22)

Did Christ really rise?

The greatest miracle in the Bible is the miracle of the resurrection. This is why so many stumble over it and find it beyond belief. Some of the explanations given for Christ's resurrection make more demands on the human mind than the actual account itself. Some maintain, for example, that it was not the real body of Jesus which rose from the dead but a ghost. It is a new thing in ghost stories which turns cowardly disciples into flaming evangelists. Others claim the disciples were so deluded that they merely *fancied* Christ had risen from the dead. The truth is that the disciples were altogether removed from the sort of mood that dreams up illusion, for instead of being excited they were stunned by sorrow. Another theory is that the enemies of Christ broke into the tomb and stole the body of Jesus under cover of darkness. If this was so, then all the enemies of Christ had to do to disprove the resurrection was to produce His body. They did not, of course, because they could not. A final theory claims that the friends of Christ rifled the tomb and removed the corpse. But how could those frightened disciples overpower Roman guards, break Caesar's seal, and then foist upon mankind a wicked fraud? Such a theory does not fit the facts; neither does it satisfy human reason.

6

● Bible References

"In the beginning God. . . ."

(GEN. 1:1)

"The fool hath said in his heart, There is no God."

(PS. 14:1)

"Who is this that darkeneth counsel by words without knowledge? . . . Where wast thou when I laid the foundations of the earth. . . ?"

(JOB 32:2, 4)

"For the truth about God is known . . . instinctively. God has put this knowledge in their hearts. Since earliest times men have seen the earth and sky and all God made, and have known of his existence and great and eternal power. So they will have no excuse. . . ."

(ROM. 1:19–20, TLB)

"O Lord my God, many and many a time you have done great miracles for us, and we are ever in your thoughts. Who else can do such glorious things? No one else can be compared with you. There isn't time to tell of all your wonderful deeds."

(PS. 40:5, TLB)

How can miracles be possible?

You must consider very carefully what lies behind this question or else you will waste a good deal of time discussing issues such as "Did Christ actually walk on the water?" or "How could He feed five thousand people with only five loaves and two fishes?" The real issue behind this question is whether or not God exists, and the questioner is really having a problem not so much with miracles but with the fact of the existence of God. If God exists, then by definition He is all-powerful, and anyone believing in the existence of God will have no problem with accepting the miraculous. There are many arguments you can present for the existence of God, but the most telling is what is known as the argument from design. Put your wristwatch (or borrow one if you don't possess one) into the hands of the questioner and say, "How long do you think it would take for that wristwatch to come together of its own accord?" You can proceed from there to show that a design needs a designer, and in the same way an orderly creation must, of necessity, have a Creator. Point out that, in fact, the Creator came to this earth 2000 years ago in the form of Jesus Christ to show us what He was like. Explain then that the only way to know God is through His Son, Jesus Christ.

● Bible References

"And we know that all things work together for good to them that love God, to them who are the called according to his purpose. For whom he did foreknow, he also did predestinate to be conformed to the image of his son. . . ."

(ROM. 8:28–29)

"My thoughts are not your thoughts, neither are your ways my ways, saith the Lord. For as the heavens are higher than the earth, so are my ways higher than your ways and my thoughts than your thoughts."

(ISA. 55:8–9)

"He restoreth my soul . . . Yea, though I walk through the valley of the shadow of death . . . thou art with me."

(PS. 23:3–4)

"And though . . . worms destroy this body, yet in my flesh shall I see God."

(JOB 19:26)

"I will restore to you the years that the locust hath eaten."

(JOEL 2:25)

"Shall not the judge of all the earth do right?"
(GEN. 18:25)

Why does God allow suffering?

Pain, accidents, death, natural tragedies, etc., raise questions that cause some people a great deal of personal anguish. In the beginning God created a perfect world, but sin quickly damaged its potential and brought disruption to all parts of God's universe. Because of the nature of the universe, sin and suffering spread to affect life in all its various forms. To those who say, "Why doesn't God just stamp out evil?" ask this question: "If at midnight tonight, God decreed that all evil would be stamped out of the universe, how many of us would be here at 12:01?" God could obliterate all evil and suffering in the world by one single stroke, but all that would prove is how much bigger and stronger He is. Instead, He has allowed it to remain in order to demonstrate not merely the attribute of power but that of wisdom and grace and how these can work through evil and suffering to glorify His Name. God does not, however, ask us to face evil and suffering without having first faced it himself. This He did on the cross and through that cross He now provides us with the grace and power not only to face all evil and suffering but to use it in deepening our sensitivity to life and making our characters into the image of Jesus Christ (Rom. 8:28–29). The only solution to evil and suffering is to become a Christian, and then one receives the power and insight to turn everything to good.

8

Further Reading

The following books will help you to further develop your counseling ministry:

The Psychology of Counseling by Clyde Narramore (Zondervan).

Handbook to Happiness by Charles R. Solomon (Coverdale).

Effective Counseling by Gary Collins (Creation House).

Encyclopedia of Psychological Problems by Clyde Narramore (Zondervan).

Why Christians Crack Up by Marion Nelson (Moody Press).

Competent to Counsel by Jay Adams (Presbyterian Publishing, USA).

The Christian Counselor's Manual by Jay Adams (Baker Book House).

Evidence That Demands a Verdict by Josh McDowell (Campus Crusade for Christ).

Know Why You Believe by Paul Little (Scripture Union).

Telling the Truth to Troubled People by William Backus (Bethany House Publishers).

Telling Yourself the Truth by William Backus and Marie Chapian (Bethany House Publishers).

Why Do I Do What I Don't Want to Do by William Backus and Marie Chapian (Bethany House Publishers).